THE WORLD ACCORDING TO HORSES

STEPHEN BUDIANSKY

THE WORLD ACCORDING TO

Horses

How They Run, See, and Think

Henry Holt and Company
New York

Henry Holt and Company, LLC
Publishers since 1866
115 West 18th Street
New York, New York 10011

Henry Holt is a registered
trademark of Henry Holt and Company, LLC

Published in Canada by Fitzhenry & Whiteside Ltd.,
195 Allstate Parkway, Markham, Ontario L3R 4T8.

Library of Congress Cataloging-in-Publication Data
Budiansky, Stephen.
The world according to horses: how they run, see, and think / by
Stephen Budiansky.
p.   cm.
Includes bibliographical references and index.
Summary: Discusses the interaction between people and horses, the horse
as a social animal, its intelligence, abilities to communicate, athletic
abilities, and physical evolution.
1. Horses—Behavior—Juvenile literature.   2. Horses—Psychology—
Juvenile literature.   [1. Horses.]   I. Title.
SF281.B845   2000   636.1—dc21   99-31778

ISBN 0-8050-6054-5 / First Edition—2000
Printed in the United States of America on acid-free paper. ∞
1   3   5   7   9   10   8   6   4   2

CONTENTS

THE WORLD ACCORDING TO HORSES

INTRODUCTION

I only began riding horses at the ridiculously advanced age of 22. I loved it right away, but I was also keenly aware that I was at a terrible disadvantage compared to people who had been riding all their lives. I think when people learn something in childhood, when their minds and bodies are still supple—whether it's playing baseball, or playing the piano, or riding a horse—they just soak it up almost automatically. But by the time a person is an adult, his or her mind and body are much more fixed in their ways, and learning something new takes a lot of thinking and a lot of effort. Maybe that's why I found myself wondering so much about *why* horses were doing what they were doing while I was struggling to get them to do what they were *supposed* to be doing.

Most horse people, I quickly found, didn't know the

answers to these "why" questions, either. I looked through dozens of horse books and found a lot about how to sit in the saddle and hold the reins and a lot about all the amazing ailments horses suffer from, but still no answers to the basic questions about why horses do what they do. Why do horses whinny, for example? Why do they shy at things like a jacket on the ground or a fallen log? Can a horse recognize individual horses or individual people? How good is their memory? These were the sorts of things I wanted to know.

There the matter lay until a few years ago, when I decided to spend a day at the National Library of Medicine, just outside of Washington, D.C., to see if anything had been published in scientific research journals about horses. I was amazed at what I found. Just within the last decade or so, there had been an explosion of new scientific research on horses—on things like behavior, vision, communication, evolution, and biomechanics. I was also struck by how little of this new scientific research had made its way into the horse world.

Of course, people have been training and riding horses for thousands of years without the help of science. But how much richer and deeper can our appreciation of these wonderful animals be if we do understand some of the "whys" about them. Determined to help bring these scientific findings to a wider audience, I wrote a book for adults called *The Nature of Horses*.

Part of my aim in writing this new book for younger readers is to bring some of this same sense of excitement and wonder about the "whys" of horses to what I think is the most dedicated group of horse lovers there is. But I have another aim: to bring to young readers some of the sense of excitement and wonder I feel about science itself. All too often these days science is presented as a bunch of facts handed down from on high or, worse, a bunch of unpronounceable words to be memorized. But that is not science at all. Science is above all else a *process* for ferreting out the truth. Sometimes it takes the form of simple discovery. But often it's much more like a detective story, a piecing together of seemingly unrelated clues to produce an often astonishing conclusion. In a detective story, *how* the detective figured out who did it is just as interesting as—actually, it's usually more interesting than—the bare fact of naming the culprit.

So in writing each chapter I have tried to make sure I explain what we know, but also how we know what we know. Each chapter is built around a narrative story explaining why horses do what they do; at the end of each chapter I have written a section called "How Do We Know?" that explains how scientists pieced together the evidence and how they devised some very clever experiments to answer questions that at first blush might seem absolutely impossible to answer. (Like—how could you tell if a horse that died 6,000 years ago had ever been ridden by a person?)

This book is organized a bit differently from other books about horses in one other way. Rather than starting 55 million years ago with the primitive ancestor of the horse, I decided to start the first chapter with the moment horses and people came together. The next three chapters then talk about horse behavior—the horse as a social animal, its intelligence, and its abilities to communicate. The final three chapters are about the physical evolution of the horse—its size and shape, its eyesight, and its remarkable athletic abilities.

Perhaps the most wonderful thing about science is that it is an adventure that never ends—new discoveries raise new questions to be answered. So in the hope I may inspire a few of you to take up the wonderful challenge that a life of science offers, I close with a short epilogue that mentions a few of the many mysteries about horses that remain to be solved.

ONE

The Cult of the Horse

A traveler—not that there were many in those needy and dangerous times—but a traveler making his way across the spare, windblown steppes of Ukraine 60 centuries ago might have stumbled upon an eerie sight:

A horse's hide, its head and feet still attached, hanging from a tripod of poles. On either side of the horse, standing mute guard, the hides of two dogs, their heads and limbs likewise still clinging to a decaying skin. And at the foot of the tripod, the remains of a very different sort of object, a work of simple but tidy craftsmanship—two antler tines pierced with holes through which ran a length of fraying cord.

In the thousands of years that have followed, this scene was repeated thousands of times. A dead horse, its head and limbs hanging from a skin suspended on poles, marked sacred sites across pagan Europe.

An ancient ritual, re-created here, marked sacred sites with horsehides mounted on poles.

Photo: Historical-Archaeological Experimental Center.

But this one horse, 60 centuries ago, was different. It was perhaps the very first horse ever ridden by a human being.

The Sredni Stog people, who lived north of the Black Sea in what is now Ukraine, had at first found food abundant and life relatively easy. Living on the border between grasslands and forest, they had no problems finding a rich variety of food. They hunted the plentiful forest game—red deer, wild pigs and wild cattle, beavers, hare—and gathered fish from the rivers that ran through the grassland valleys. And so things went for a thousand years or more. But about 6,600 years ago changes began upsetting this orderly way of life. Farmers and herders who came from the Danube River to the west brought new ways and new tools: domestic cattle, sheep, and pigs; wheat and barley; ceramic pottery; simple but beautiful ornaments made from hammered copper. Slowly these new influences began to spread through the region. As these new food-producing methods took hold, people became richer and their camps grew larger. People had larger families and needed larger homes. Camps became permanent villages.

But other things began to change, too. The huge forests began to disappear. They were burned and cut down to make way for pastures for domestic livestock. More trees were cleared for garden plots to grow the new crops. The once plentiful forest game dwindled.

As the forests dwindled, the hunters began to explore the steppe, the wild, open grasslands that stretched hundreds of miles without a break. And here they encountered a new animal: the horse. A wild animal of the steppe, the horse had never before been hunted by these dwellers of the forest-steppe boundary lands. Yet by 6,000 years ago the people of one site in this region, a site now known as Dereivka, were getting more than half of their meat from wild horses they hunted on the steppe. The wild horse had become even more important than domestic cattle and sheep, more important than the forest game of deer and wild pig and beaver.

In hunting the horse, these people of the Sredni Stog culture were in a way a throwback to a much earlier time.

The horse had once roamed across North America, across all of Europe and Central Asia. When glaciers covered much of the land of North America and Europe in vast sheets of ice, some a mile thick, the open land that was left

The cave paintings left by Stone Age peoples in Lascaux, France, depict many horses being hunted.

Photo: © Shelly Grossman/PNI, 1980.

south of the glaciers was grassland. Vast open expanses, treeless, windswept—this was the natural home of the horse. But beginning about 20,000 years ago the earth began to warm, following one of its many and endless cycles of climate change. Forests began to invade the grasslands. As the land warmed and the glaciers retreated, seeds blown by the wind or carried by animals took hold in soil and began to grow where no trees had grown for thousands of years. The open lands where the horse lived were shrinking. The ancient Indians of North America, whose population was growing and whose skill as hunters was growing, too, relentlessly pursued the horse and the other large animals that once roamed the continent. Huge mammoths and mastodons, giant elk, saber-toothed tigers—and horses—all vanished under this combined onslaught of humanity and nature. By 10,000 years ago, not a horse remained alive in North America.

In Europe the horse was disappearing, too. The forests swept eastward, and the horse vanished from Britain, from France and Spain, until all that was left was a remnant of a once vast herd in Ukraine and Central Asia—the only spot that still offered the horse its natural habitat of open grassland. The hunters of North America and Europe had long since turned to other game by the time the Sredni Stog people began hunting horses.

This time, though, the pattern would be broken. Everywhere else, man and nature together had sent the horse to extinction. At Dereivka, the horse—making its very last stand in its very last remaining bit of natural habitat—would be saved.

And from Dereivka something amazing happened. The horse population began to grow again and to sweep back, in what was almost a tidal wave, to the very places it had vanished from centuries before. By 4,500 to 5,000 years ago the horse reappeared in Central Europe, in what is now Hungary and Romania. By 4,000 years ago the horse returned to Britain. It would take another 3,500 years after that for the horse to return to North America, but return it would. On Christopher Columbus's second voyage to the New World he brought with him to the Caribbean island of Hispaniola (which today forms the countries of Haiti and the Dominican Republic) 24 stallions and 10 mares, arriving on January 2, 1494.

The horse was saved because now it was in the company of humans: It was domesticated. To the Sredni Stog people, the horse was a valuable source of food for the harsh winters in a land where once familiar sources of food were gone. They had sheep and cattle, but feeding sheep and cattle in the winter was difficult in the extreme. Heavy blankets of snow covered the ground, and the number of animals that would survive the winter depended on how much forage could be collected for them. Horses had a special advantage, though. The horse, unlike cattle and sheep, paws through snow to find grass. The horse can eat a diet that would cause a cow or sheep to starve to death. Horses were a way for the people of this now harsh land to store meat on the hoof for the winter.

But horses were also something else. For as soon as the horse entered the society of humans, human life changed in a fashion almost unequaled in history. Sometime during one of those short winter days, or perhaps in the spring, when the horses began shedding their coats and sought out something to scratch their itchy necks and backs against, one particularly brave or one particularly foolhardy person leapt upon the back of a horse that came near. The swiftness of the horse was now ours to share.

Warriors on horseback were an unimaginable threat to neighboring peoples. The horse brought a new form of swift and often terrible warfare. It transformed the deep steppe, once a barrier to humans and a land too sparse in resources to live on, into a place that could be crossed and exploited. The horse became a means of transport eastward across the steppe to Asia. Men on horseback could also cover a vast area to hunt and to pasture their livestock. The fact that grass grew only sparsely and game was rare mattered much less, for one person on a horse could cover in a day an area of land perhaps six times as great as a person on foot.

To protect themselves against these newly powerful and newly mobile people of the horse, other people began to build ever larger and better-fortified villages. Some villages were abandoned entirely. Men could now appear without warning and sweep down upon a village to plunder its wealth and stores of food, galloping off into the trackless steppe as quickly as they had come. Staying in one place no longer was possible. In self-defense, many villagers became mounted nomads and hunters themselves.

The horse transformed trade. Villages that were once isolated were now in touch over hundreds of miles. Exotic goods began to make their way to remote spots. The new wealth and the new warfare and the new ways of life the horse brought sped up the emergence of social rank, with the rich and powerful—and few—at the top, and the many and less well-off at the bottom.

Finally, the horse changed even the way people spoke. As the Sredni Stog and other peoples of the grasslands of Ukraine traveled east and west in the company of the horse, they took their language with them. It was an ancestor of the languages of the Indo-European family, which would include the ancient tongues of Greek, Latin, and Sanskrit—and most modern European languages, including English.

Starting in that one faraway spot long ago, the horse came back from the very brink of extinction to populate the world in the company of humans. It is no exaggeration to say that nothing has been the same since. The horse changed the way people lived and fought and the way they worked and played; the horse changed the way people spoke and what they thought of and knew about the world beyond their village; the horse changed the way people became rich and powerful—or poor and enslaved.

How Do We Know?

How could you tell, by looking at the bones of a horse, if it had ever been ridden?

How could you tell if a horse was domesticated—that is, raised in captivity by people—or if it was still a wild animal?

How could you tell if a horse had been used as food or kept to ride?

When archaeologists digging at Dereivka found the skull and left front leg of a horse, together with the skeletons of two dogs and some scraps of pottery and antlers, they didn't have much to go on. But they knew right away that something was unusual about this particular set of bones and objects.

At other sites in the area, they had found thousands of horse bones. These other sites also contained the bones of many other food animals, such as deer and cattle. Such heaps of bones were similar to the heaps of bones that archaeologists have unearthed in many, many places where ancient humans lived. Archaeologists call these kitchen middens; they are basically garbage dumps, where people brought the animals they had killed and butchered and cooked and ate them.

At Dereivka archaeologists could count the number of bones of different animals in each of these kitchen middens and figure out what the people who lived there ate. It requires a lot of training and practice to identify an animal from one of its bones—often just from a scrap of a bone. But to a practiced eye a horse leg bone looks very different from a cow or a deer leg bone. By examining different sites where people lived in different periods, the archaeologists could also figure out how the people's diet changed over time. That is how scientists were able to discover the sudden shift from forest game to the horse that took place in the area around Dereivka about 6,000 years ago.

The horse skull they found, however, was clearly something different. The very fact that it was a skull, and was together with a leg, was odd. The jaw of the horse doesn't have much meat on it, so very few skulls were brought back to the camps where the meat was cooked and eaten. This skull, in other words, did not appear to have come from a horse that had been killed and eaten at all.

The most significant clue, though, was that the horse and the two dogs were carefully arranged in a group, along with small clay statues and other man-made objects. Scientists knew from reports as recent as the early twentieth century that people who lived in Central Asia practiced a ritual custom of mounting horsehides on poles to mark sacred sites. This site at Dereivka seemed to match exactly those descriptions. Scientists also knew that across ancient Europe, one old legend told of a horse that bears the souls of dead men to the gates of Hades, where dogs stand guard. The grouping of a horse and dogs that they found at the site seemed to be a ritual reenactment of that legend.

This horse, then, might have been sacrificed as part of a religious ritual. But there were other small clues that suggested a deeper meaning and significance. The two pieces of antler with holes bored in them looked very much like objects that had been found elsewhere in Europe, at sites from about 2,000 years later. At those sites the evidence is very strong that these objects were used as the cheekpieces of a bridle—the pieces of the bridle that rest on either side of the horse's mouth, which the bit runs between. Pictures from these later sites show such cheekpieces used with a rope bit running through the holes.

This still fell short of complete proof that the Dereivka horse had been ridden. But David Anthony, an American archaeologist who had studied the findings at Dereivka, came up with an ingenious way to test this question. When a horse has a bit in its mouth, the bit normally rests in the space between the front teeth and the back molar teeth. That gap doesn't exist in people, but it does in horses. A properly placed bit works by pressing against the sensitive, soft tissues in this gap. A small pull on the reins is all that it takes to control a well-trained horse.

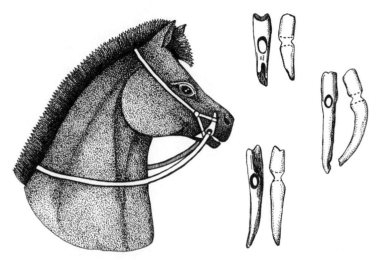

Pieces of antler with holes bored through them were used as the cheekpieces for rope bridles.

But Anthony talked to veterinarians and discovered that it's actually very hard to adjust a bit so it sits right where it is supposed to. Some veterinarians had actually taken x-ray movies of bits inside a horse's mouth. What they found was that horses often use their tongue to pull the bit back and then bite down on the bit with their teeth.

Anthony realized this could be a very powerful tool to tell if a horse had ever had a bit in its mouth. He looked at teeth of horses that he knew had never been ridden—wild horses from Assateague Island in Virginia and from Nevada. He looked at teeth from racehorses. (All of the horses had died of natural causes and were being studied in veterinary hospitals.) When he examined the teeth under a very powerful microscope called a scanning electron microscope, which magnified the image 2,000 times, Anthony found that the

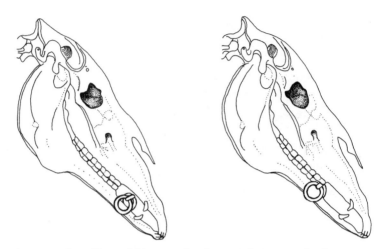

A properly adjusted bit rests in the gap between the front and the back teeth (left). But horses often chew on the bit (right), which leaves telltale marks on the teeth. Below, left to right, the teeth of the Dereivka stallion, a modern race-horse, and a feral stallion.

racehorse teeth all had small cracks and wear patterns. None of the teeth from the wild horses did.

Then came the test: Would the Dereivka horse have these same wear patterns on its teeth? It did. That was convincing evidence that this horse from 6,000 years ago had carried a bit in its mouth.

Other research has shown that the first wheels did not appear anywhere in the world for another 500 years. So five centuries before the invention of the wheel, a horse had been bridled. If it could not have been pulling a cart, it was almost certainly ridden.

But was the horse first domesticated at Dereivka as a source of meat or to be ridden? Teeth tell a story here, too. Horses' teeth are unusual in one way: They keep growing throughout an animal's life. As they grow, they change shape in a predictable way. Scientists looking at a horse's tooth can calculate with a fair degree of accuracy how old it is. So by looking at the teeth in an archaeological site, they can figure out how old the horse was when it died.

In the bones left from a population of wild horses, where death comes from natural causes, you would expect to find a lot of teeth from young horses less than a few years old. In the wild, these young animals are especially vulnerable to disease and being attacked by predators. There would be few teeth from animals in the prime of life and more from animals that die from old age.

The bones of wild horses that had been hunted would tell a very different story. The best animals for a hunter to kill would be those in the prime of life—young animals don't have enough meat on them, and the flesh of older ones would be tough.

And finally, the bones of a domestic herd raised for meat would be different again. Here, most of the animals killed would be two- or three-year-olds. In captivity a breeder doesn't want to keep a lot of mature adults, especially males. He needs to keep only a few for breeding and so would cull a lot of animals just as they reach sexual maturity.

Scientist Marsha Levine realized that by collecting all the horse teeth from Dereivka and making a graph showing how many there were from each age group, she might be able to tell whether the Dereivka horses were wild animals that were hunted or tame animals raised for meat. The closest fit turned out to be with what you would expect for wild animals that were hunted. Most of the teeth were from animals between five and eight years old.

That suggests that at the time the Sredni Stog people were eating a lot of horses, they were hunting them in the wild. When they finally domesticated the horse, it was not as a source of food, but as a mount to be ridden.

But there is one odd thing about the data. There seem to be a lot more males than females in the Dereivka kitchen middens. Male horses have canine teeth that females lack, so it's possible to tell them apart if you find an entire jaw with the teeth in place. That would suggest that Dereivka horses were domesticated as a meat source first and only later ridden.

More research may finally settle this question.

TWO

Horse Society

People domesticated horses; had they not, the horse would almost surely be extinct. But the horse deserves credit, too, for this feat. For in a way, horses actually domesticated themselves. Long before horses ever began to associate with humans, they had developed certain traits that predisposed them to a life with us. Horses are intensely social animals. Many of the behaviors they show toward us are behaviors that they evolved in order to deal with the demands of living with other horses.

For example, if you stand in front of a horse and scratch him on his neck for a while, he will sometimes reach forward with his head and begin gently scratching your shoulder or back with his teeth. This is a well-known ritual in the horse world. Two horses stand side by side, head to tail, and "groom" each other's neck and back. It is a use-

Horses cement bonds of friendship within the herd through mutual grooming.

ful ritual, because a horse cannot reach many parts of its body with its own mouth; having another horse scratch you where you can't scratch yourself makes perfect sense.

But it is also ritual that helps cement bonds of friendship within the herd. To allow another horse to invade one's own "personal space" is an act of trust, because horses normally protect a region around themselves. They will move away from—or threaten—anyone or anything that gets too near. When grooming each other, a pair of horses lowers its guard.

That horses will extend this show of trust to their owners is a sign of just how much people are accepted by the horse into its world: Horses think of us as members of the herd.

Indeed, people get along best with horses when they are accepted as a friend—a member of the herd. But not necessarily as an equal. Horses have a well-defined social structure based on rank. And the secret of having a horse that obeys us without a fight or a continual struggle is to have a horse that accepts us as *high-ranking* members of the horse herd.

In horse society, individuals can be both friends and bosses at the same time. Friendship is what glues the entire herd together. Every horse within the herd will at one time or another groom every other horse. Very often, after two horses have had a hostile encounter, they will "make up" by grooming each other. It is a ritual that binds every member of the group to every other. In the wild, the only horses that never groom one another are members of different herds or the young foals and the dominant stallion within one herd.

At the same time, horse society is one in which everyone knows who the bosses are. Horses at the top of the social order—the dominant members of the herd—have first access to food or water or preferred places.

Horses have a complex system of establishing who is at the top of the heap. As animals that evolved in the open grasslands, where there are no trees to block the view, they rely very naturally on visual signals. These signals are all closely related to aggression. Yet in actual day-to-day encounters between horses, acts of true violence are rare. What horses have evolved is a system of pantomime aggression. Instead of kicking another horse, a horse may just cock its hind leg as if to start a kick. Instead of biting another horse, a horse may lower its head and reach out as if to bite. Instead of striking with its front leg, it will merely lift its hoof.

The most aggressive threats are those used by stallions against the stallions of another herd. Mostly, bands of horses try to avoid one another. When stallions do meet, they sometimes fight. But before that happens, they will engage in often long contests of threats and posturing and bluffs. Stallions will raise and lower their heads several times in a row. They will prance in a circle. They will stomp the ground with their front hoof. They will also engage in lengthy squealing contests.

Often one stallion will move off after these mock fights. Apparently horses can judge accurately how likely they are to win or lose a real fight from these pantomime perfor-

Actual fights between stallions are comparatively rare; far more common are mock fights and squealing contests.

Photo: © Jeff Foott/PNI, 1994.

mances and so give way rather than risk a genuine physical confrontation if the odds are against them.

Within a band, threatening gestures are often employed whenever horses compete for a favored spot near food or water. Some are as subtle as laying back the ears. Other times a dominant horse will move its hindquarters into a position where it *could* kick another horse (even though it doesn't).

Submissive horses respond by moving away or by adopting a number of postures that also act as signals of bowing to a higher-ranking horse. They will turn their head slightly away from a threat. They will tuck their tail tightly against their body.

One of the most common threats used by herd stallions to get the other horses of the group to move is a "herding" posture, in which the stallion lowers his head and neck and moves toward the other horses. In herds of feral horses, stallions are able to get the mares to move 98 percent of the time by doing nothing more than lowering their heads in this fashion.

Flattening the ears is one of the most common signals of a threat by a horse. Ears are a vulnerable part of a horse's body. A horse intending to fight another will instinctively protect its vulnerable parts in preparation for a physical encounter.

Over many generations of evolution, such a physical gesture can become ritualized. What began as an actual motion used in a fight turns into a system of communication. In a group-dwelling animal like the horse, it is in nobody's interest ever to come to blows. Even the winner in a fight risks injury, and in the wild, serious injury is usually a death sentence. If a dominant horse can get his way without fighting, he is far better off. And likewise, if a lower-ranking horse can avoid a fight he would lose anyway, he is going to survive better than if he fights. So it pays for a lower-ranking horse to learn to recognize signs of impending trouble. In generations past, low-ranking horses that ran away from horses with lowered ears tended to be the low-ranking horses that survived to pass on that skill to the next generation. Likewise, high-ranking horses that exploited this fact—by just lowering their ears when they wanted another horse to move rather than by immediately launching an attack with no warning—were more likely to survive and pass on *that* trait.

Skillful human trainers put all of this to good use when they work with horses. A horse that directly challenges a trainer with an aggressive threat or an actual kick or bite must usually be swiftly put in its place. In those circumstances, the horse is directly challenging the human's status at the top of the social ranking. But good trainers know that the occasions when they have to use physical force are rare. Often one whack of a crop on the horse's flank is all that's required. After that, trainers can exploit the horse's natural ability to "read" visual signals. The mere *threat* of physical force is all that's needed to keep the social rankings where they need to be. A trainer working with a horse on a long lead can get the horse to move by moving toward it. A sharp tone of voice—or even just holding a crop in one's hand—is often all that a rider needs to get a well-trained horse to obey commands without a fight.

Humans can reinforce the "friendship" bonds with their horses through such activities as grooming. When you brush a horse, the horse is accepting you just as it accepts its herd mates. It is allowing you to violate its personal space. There is some scientific evidence that grooming a horse reduces its tension and stimulates an automatic, pleasurable response. Horses most often groom each other on the lower neck. When horses are brushed at this place by a person, their heart rate decreases 10 percent or more. (Brushing at places horses never groom, such as the elbow, has no effect on heart rate.) A major bundle of nerves runs very close to the lower neck, which may explain why grooming at this site has this effect.

Scratching and petting a horse is an effective way to communicate praise. It is also a basic ingredient in the social glue that binds horses to us.

One way young horses learn to become regular members of horse society is through play. Foals engage in pretend fights with one another and charge about in groups. Foals seem to learn new things very quickly when they are first born. Within hours of birth they learn to follow their mothers. Within the first few weeks they adapt to new experiences rapidly. This kind of learning is called *imprinting* and seems to be an adaptation to life peculiar to many animals whose young are able to move on their own shortly after birth. Foals, indeed, are able to stand and run within hours of birth. They thus have little time to learn who their

*Through grooming and other social interactions, horses
come to accept humans as fellow members of the herd.*

mother is before they are moving with the whole herd. So they have an instinct to form a fast and tight bond with the first moving thing they encounter after birth. Horses that are hand-reared by a human will imprint just as surely on that person as they would on their natural mother.

Some trainers use imprint training—not to get foals to imprint on them, which actually can create behavioral problems—but to expose them to new experiences as soon as possible. Things like having its feet handled, having a bit placed in its mouth, going into a horse trailer, and hearing loud noises are all potentially very frightening to a horse. A foal that is repeatedly exposed to these experiences as soon as possible rapidly learns to view them as just a natural part of its environment. The foal then accepts them much more readily than it would if it first encountered them only years later, when its regular training begins.

How Do We Know?

How do we know what horse signals "mean"?

How do we know that horses have different "ranks" within the herd?

Most of what we know about horses' social life comes from field studies of wild horses. Horse researcher Joel Berger spent 509 hours watching the horse herds of the Grand Canyon from March to August of one year. He traveled across an area of about 150 square miles on foot and on a motorcycle and used powerful binoculars and a movie camera to observe and record the horses' actions. Berger identified individual horses by their color and markings.

To pin down the social ranking of the horses in each band, Berger watched what happened as the members of several herds came to drink at the one water hole in the region. This was a spring near the top of a steep hill about 180 feet high. A small ledge about 25 feet farther up the hill gave Berger a perfect outpost for watching the horses' interactions when they came to drink. This spring was shared among four different bands of horses that moved throughout the area and so was the major place where these different groups encountered one another—because normally they tended to stay out of one another's way. Since water is scarce in this area, and since the spring was small and always had only one best spot for drinking— where the water was deepest—the horses who came to drink would always compete with one another to get into that best spot. So it was a ready-made place to observe the battle for social rank within and among herds.

Berger tallied a total of 947 exchanges of threats between horses at the spring. He carefully recorded how many times each horse would threaten which other horses and how many times each horse succeeded in making another horse move away from the preferred spot. In one band, for example, the stallion was dominant in 123 encounters and subordinate in one. Mare A had a total "win-loss" score of 30–52; Mare B, 25–50; Mare C, 21–78; the single foal was zero for 18. That ranking held all the way down the line, with Mare A beating Mare C 26–17, and Mare B beating Mare C 17–3.

A herd of feral horses.   Photo: © Wolfgang Bayer/PNI, 1994.

Berger also carefully monitored and recorded the reper-
toire of behaviors a horse would go through in an aggressive
encounter. He observed that a horse would progress
through three escalating phases. The first stage consisted of
what he called "prethreats." A horse would try to get another
to move by turning its hind end toward the other horse, by
bobbing its head up and down, or by using its whole body to
body block the other horse. If the target of these prethreats
moved off, that ended the conflict. If it did not move, the first
horse would usually escalate to a more clearly expressed
threat. Such threats included lifting a rear leg, pinning back
the ears and lowering the head, or attempting to bite (but
missing). Only when these threats failed would a horse
escalate to actual physical contact—kicking with the hind
legs, striking with the forelegs, or biting.

One interesting thing Berger found was that the rank orders were remarkably stable within the bands. Throughout the six months he watched the horses, the rank order never changed. In other words, once horses find their place in the social structure, they are usually comfortable staying there.

And actual physical conflict is indeed rare. Among free-ranging horses studied on the Scottish island of Rhum, 80 percent of threatening encounters consisted of threats with the head alone. Kick threats, or actual kicks or bites, seldom occurred.

Although the threat of violence is ever present within a herd of horses, social rank is really a way to keep the peace.

THREE

Horse Smarts

Lady Wonder was a horse that lived in Virginia in the 1920s. Her owner made headlines by announcing to the world that Lady Wonder had a remarkable ability: She could read minds. People would whisper a question to Lady Wonder's owner, and Lady Wonder would then answer it by moving wooden blocks with her nose to spell out words. A prominent professor of psychology—who, unfortunately, did not know very much about horses—came to investigate the phenomenon and was so impressed that he wrote a scholarly article describing this example of animal ESP.

Finally, however, someone who knew a bit more about both animals and human trickery decided to look into the matter. He was John Scarne, a professional magician. Magicians, of course, know that things aren't always what they seem to be. After all, they make a living by tricking people into thinking they have seen things that they really haven't.

Professional magicians perform tricks to entertain and amaze. What bothered Scarne was that some hucksters were performing magic tricks and making all sorts of preposterous claims about occult powers or psychic abilities—and often getting gullible people to part with hundreds or thousands of dollars in search of "spiritual" guidance from these pretend psychics.

So Scarne investigated Lady Wonder's performance and noticed something very interesting: Whenever Lady Wonder moved the blocks, her owner was standing behind her holding a whip. Scarne finally figured out what was happening. Lady Wonder's owner had trained her to respond to small movements of his whip as signals. He was picking out which blocks Lady Wonder was to move and secretly signaling her.

Part of what had fooled the university professor was that he thought Lady Wonder's owner was standing so far behind the horse that there was no way Lady Wonder could see him. He didn't know that horses can see almost directly behind themselves without turning their head.

Horses cannot read our minds. But they often act as if they do. Many riders have had the experience of their horse being aware when they are nervous or tense. A rider who starts to think about jumping over a fence that's not even in sight yet may find that his horse becomes suddenly excited and starts galloping toward the spot. By the same token, many beautifully trained horses will learn to change from a

walk to a trot or execute other much more intricate maneu-
vers in response to signals from their rider that seem completely invisible to someone watching.

How do horses do these things? The basic answer is that
horses, as social animals, are extremely adept at picking up
on the smallest signals. The smallest squeeze of the legs by
their riders—even a slight tensing of the rider's muscles—is
a signal that a horse can detect. You may not even be aware
that you're tensing your muscles, but your horse often is.
That's why when you're nervous, or when you think about
that fence ahead and start to get a little bit excited yourself,
your horse can tell.

Horses are very good at forming mental connections
between signals and actions. That's a basic survival skill all
animals have. If certain actions on their part lead to a bad
result, they learn to avoid doing that. A horse that was
scared at a certain spot where a dog jumped out from
behind a tree will often shy away from that spot. Likewise,
an action that leads to a good result will be remembered,
too. Horses very quickly learn that a person carrying a
bucket is bringing food.

Training a horse is a process of giving it the chance to
form a connection in its mind between signals that we
invent and actions we want it to carry out. Much of our
training of horses uses what psychologists call *negative
reinforcement*. A lot of people misunderstand what "negative" means in this case—it doesn't mean punishment. Positive reinforcement means giving a positive reward (like
food or a pat on the neck) for doing the right thing. Negative

reinforcement means taking away something unpleasant as the reward for doing the right thing. When you say "walk" to your horse and then squeeze with your legs, the squeeze is something slightly unpleasant. As soon as the horse starts to move forward, you stop squeezing—that is the reward for its correct response. Likewise, when you pull on the reins to get your horse to stop and then release the pressure on the reins when it responds, that is another example of negative reinforcement: You are providing a reward by removing something unpleasant.

Much of training also involves substituting one signal for another. You might first teach a horse to walk on command by flicking its rump lightly with a whip. The horse learns to associate the signal (a flick of the whip) with its action (starting to move). Training that replaces one signal with another is called *trace conditioning*. The process that works is to give the new signal (you might say the word *walk* out loud, for example), then use the old signal (a flick of the whip). Horses usually learn very quickly to associate the new signal with the previously learned action this way. Giving the new and old signals at the same time, however, does not work to teach the new signal. Nor does giving the old signal first and then the new one. Neither of those methods gives the horse the chance to make the connection between cause and effect that is the basis of learning.

Because horses so readily learn to form associations between things in their environment and because they are so good at perceiving very subtle signals, they learn bad habits easily. That is part of what makes riding so challenging an art. A rider has to be very aware of his own body to avoid unconsciously giving the horse inadvertent signals that can undo its training. For example, a rider who does not use his hands well can, without realizing it, "teach" his horse to be very stubborn. If the rider pulls back on the reins every time he goes over a jump, a horse can quickly learn to associate jumping with something unpleasant— getting banged in the mouth—and may discover that stopping short right before the jump is a way to avoid this. A horse that gets away with evading a command (like walking when told to canter or cutting across a ring rather than moving along the edge) has in effect been rewarded for it— and will often repeat this behavior.

Likewise, many horses that misbehave do so because their riders, without realizing it, have been rewarding them for this behavior. If a horse that acts up and starts bucking or disobeying commands discovers that every time it does so its rider gets off and takes it back to its stable, the horse doesn't have to be a genius to form this connection between its (mis)behavior and the resulting reward—getting this person off its back and going back home.

Horses have another characteristic that is both a boon and a bane to riders: They have excellent memories, for both good and bad lessons learned.

Punishment is a two-edged sword in training. On the one hand, it can be necessary in cases of serious disobedience to reinforce the rider's or trainer's position of social dominance. But it is less effective in teaching a horse a new command. Horses can become so worried about being punished for making a mistake that they become hesitant and indecisive.

How Do We Know?

How do we know that horses can detect almost invisible social signals from other animals?

How do we know that horses have good memories?

How do we know that horses can become nervous about getting the right answer when they are punished for mistakes?

Lady Wonder was a hoax: Her owner deliberately tried to fool people and had very carefully trained her to obey signals. But another famous horse from the early twentieth century provided an even more sobering lesson about how readily horses can learn to associate very small social signals with their own actions.

Clever Hans was a horse who lived in Berlin. His owner was no trickster but an earnest, sober, respectable retired schoolmaster named Wilhelm von Osten. Perhaps because he was a schoolmaster, von Osten decided to treat Hans as one of his pupils. He taught him to add and subtract, to identify pieces of money and musical scores, and to answer questions about geography and world leaders. Hans would answer the mathematical questions by stomping his foot the correct number of times. He would answer other questions by shaking or nodding his head. Von Osten would give Hans a reward of a sugar cube for getting the right answer. And

Clever Hans did math and answered questions about geography. In fact, he was just responding to unconscious signals from his questioners.

before long Hans was displaying a dazzling knowledge of arithmetic, world affairs, and many other subjects.

Did Hans really know these things? And if he didn't know them, how come he got the right answers so consistently? The solution to this mystery came from a commission of distinguished scientists who were sent to investigate Hans's mental powers. They first did the obvious experiment—they sent von Osten out of the room and tried asking Hans the questions themselves. Someone would ask Hans how much four plus three was, and sure enough, Hans would stomp his foot seven times.

But they still suspected that Hans didn't actually know these things—that somehow, without even being aware of it, the people in the room were giving Hans a signal of when to stop stomping his foot. So they tried a very clever second experiment. They had one person go up to Hans and whisper one number into his ear. Then a second person whispered a second number to Hans. The people did not tell each other what number each had given Hans. So no one in the room—except Hans!—even knew what the addition problem was. When the scientists tried this, Hans's ability to perform mathematics completely vanished. He would stomp his foot, but only rarely got the right answer.

What was happening was this: When they knew the answer to the problem that Hans had been given, even the scientists were unconsciously giving Hans a cue. Hans would start stomping his foot, and the people in the room would become slightly more tense as he approached the right number. When he got to the right number, they would slightly relax or sigh or do something that Hans had learned to recognize. Having been repeatedly rewarded with a sugar cube for stomping his foot and then stopping when that (unconscious) signal was given, Hans had no trouble doing what he would get a reward for.

Experiments with other horses have shown that they have excellent memories and can learn to distinguish between many sorts of cues—whether those cues involve sight, sound, or feel. In one experiment, a horse was shown a series of 20 pairs of panels with designs on them. In one pair, the first panel might have a letter *L* and the second panel a letter *R*. In another pair, the choice might be a squiggly line or a dash, or a plus sign and a dot, or a picture of a bird and a picture of a bug. In each pair, choosing one would earn the horse a small food reward, and choosing the other would result in nothing happening. The horse was shown the 20 pairs over and over until it learned to consistently choose the one of each pair that produced the reward. When the horse was retested even a year later, it was able to remember all of the correct answers with a high degree of accuracy.

Experiments in which horses were punished for choosing the wrong answer have shown how punishment can backfire. In one test, horses were led into a simple maze. They had to choose to turn either to the right or to the left. If they went the correct way, they would come around a corner to an open door leading out to a field where other horses were. If they went the wrong way, they would come around a corner and face a solid wall and have to retrace their steps.

The researchers then tried a slight modification of the experiment. Horses that chose the wrong turn were met with a blast from a fire extinguisher. The fire extinguisher made a noise and blew some harmless carbon dioxide gas at the horse.

The results were interesting: The horses in this modified experiment did learn faster than horses in the first experiment. They made fewer wrong choices. But they also took a lot longer to make their choice each time. They would enter the maze and stand for a long time before turning either left or right. It was as if they became much more worried about getting the right answer. Experiments like these show that horses learn best and with the fewest bad side effects (such as hesitation) when they are given a clear choice of responses and are consistently rewarded for the right choice.

FOUR

Sounding Off

Once when the stallion Triangle and the rest of his band had moved off from the water hole, Goldylocks and her foal Gold stayed behind. By the time Goldylocks and Gold were through drinking their fill, their band was already out of sight about a quarter mile away.

Goldylocks let out a long whinny. Triangle immediately brought the herd to a halt and waited for Goldylocks and Gold to catch up.

This same scene was repeated more than once. Although these were feral horses living freely on the rangelands of Wyoming and Montana, the way Goldylocks used the whinny to communicate over a long distance to another horse who was out of sight is instantly familiar to all horse owners. Two stablemates that are separated will frequently whinny to each other. It is easy for us to think that a whinny has a meaning that we might put into words as "Wait for me!"

But horses whinny in lots of other circumstances, too. A mare will respond to its whinnying foal by whinnying back and searching for it. In the wild, stallions in different bands will whinny to each other in order to find out where they are—and stay out of each other's way. A stabled horse that is extremely hungry, or frustrated by being kept in a stall, will whinny when its owner approaches the barn. A horse that has been left in the barn when its stablemate is taken out for a ride will often whinny when its companion leaves and when it returns.

What would the "meaning" for each of these kinds of whinnies be? It might be "Stay out of my way," or "Come and get me," or "Don't go," or "Welcome back." Yet exactly the same sound is used in all of these cases.

Which means there is probably something wrong with trying to assign specific meanings to horse sounds in the first place. Horses are clearly communicating with one another when they whinny. But it's a kind of communication that is very different from language. Horse sounds are not words or sentences. They are something else entirely.

In human language, the meaning of a sound has nothing to do with the type of sound it is. A few words, of course, are imitations of sounds—like *boom!* or *crackle* or *woof.* But most are just chance combinations of vowels and consonants. Different languages use completely different sounds to mean the same thing. There is nothing magical about particular sounds that make them stand for particular things.

The key to understanding horse communication, though, is that the texture and tone of a sound is very closely connected with the way it is used.

What is it about the sound of a whinny that can tell us why horses use this sound in certain circumstances? To start with, one characteristic of the whinny is that it's a very individual sound. Each horse has a distinctive whinny. Mares can tell whether a whinny is from their foal or a different foal just from the sound.

The other special characteristic of a whinny is that it's made up of sound waves that can travel a very long distance. In open environments, a sound that is relatively low pitched and "buzzy" tends to travel much farther than other kinds of sounds. That is precisely the characteristic of the whinny.

So whinnies are a way of identifying oneself to another horse (or occasionally a person!) that is out of sight. A horse's whinny is shaped more by the laws of acoustics—how sounds are generated and travel—than by any precise wordlike meaning.

Horses make a number of other sounds that are closely matched to their environment and to limits set by the laws of acoustics. The whinny is designed to travel through air effectively and still be audible a long distance away. The nicker is designed to travel through a very different medium. A nicker is a very low, gentle vibrating sound that horses in barns will often use as a greeting for their owners—especially at feeding time. In the wild, horses will use this to greet a "friend," and stallions will use it when approaching a mare as part of their courtship rituals.

Most of all, the nicker is used between foals and their mothers. If we were to try to assign precise meanings to this sound, we would have to call it a greeting call, a mating call, and a nursing-young call all at once. It turns out that the nicker is a sound that travels best not through the air at all, but directly through an animal's body. This is probably because it originated to serve the function that it's still most commonly used for—communication between a mare and its foal. A foal that is nursing can make this sound and it travels directly through the mare's body, where it is more *felt* than heard.

Just as certain physical motions in horses have now become part of a ritual (lifting a leg instead of actually kicking, for example), so this sound has taken on a broader purpose. There is nothing less threatening than a foal. So a horse that wants to communicate its nonaggressive intentions can use a nicker, and its meaning will be automatically understood. A hungry horse that uses this sound to its owner may be mimicking the nursing call of a young horse. Domestic horses are in some ways more juvenile in their behavior than their wild forebears probably were—they tend to retain into adulthood certain youthful traits, especially dependence and the sort of food-begging habits that many baby mammals (and birds, too) exhibit.

One of the more unusual horse sounds is what is sometimes called the "blow." The horse will exhale sharply through its nose. But it turns out that this kind of sound is not at all unusual in the animal kingdom. In terms of the way the sound rises and falls in both pitch and loudness, it's exactly like a dog's bark.

Horses use this sound much like dogs use a bark, too. They will blow when they spot something in their environment that interests them and that they are not yet sure how to react to. When one horse blows, other horses in the area will usually turn and look in the same direction. In a sense, then, blowing is a way to recruit the other members of the herd to pay attention. If the something turns out to be threatening, many eyes are better than two to keep watch on it. So it is very much in the interests of the "blower" to get help.

Why should this call have the acoustic property of rising and falling in pitch? One explanation is that all barklike sounds are actually halfway sounds—halfway between a growl that conveys a sense of being threatening and a whine that conveys a sense of being appeasing. Many animals automatically recognize this code. That's probably because small things naturally make high-pitched sounds and big things make low-pitched sounds. (That's a law of acoustics, too. A long organ pipe or string makes a lower sound than a short pipe or string.) An animal tends to use a low sound to communicate a hostile intent because it's automatically threatening—since big things really *are* threatening. Likewise, a whine, a small, high-pitched sound, is automatically nonthreatening.

The bark is a deliberately neutral sound. It lets whatever is out there know it's been spotted, but without expressing any hostile intention (the way a growl would) or surrender (the way a whine would). That is a prudent policy for an animal to follow when it encounters something unknown. A carelessly uttered threat or surrender might provoke an attack. A bark is studiously noncommittal.

If horses bark, why don't they whine or growl? It may be in part because so much of their communication about hostility and submission is done visually. It's interesting that some close relatives of the horse, including the forest-dwelling tapir and some species of zebra, make high-pitched whistles or squeaks that seem to function like whines. But the horse, having evolved in the open grasslands and living in bands that tend to stay close together, finds visual communication in many ways better suited to its way of life.

Although horses don't make sounds that correspond exactly to a whine or a growl, they do seem to recognize these sounds and understand their sense. A sharp word addressed to a disobedient horse in a harsh, low-pitched tone can serve as an effective correction. Likewise, horses seem to recognize a soft, high-pitched tone of voice as inherently nonthreatening. Since so many creatures in the world *do* make such sounds, it is sensible that horses have acquired over the course of evolution an ability to interpret them correctly. Avoiding big or hostile creatures has clear survival value. Not wasting energy running away from small or nonthreatening creatures has survival value, too.

How Do We Know?

How do we know that a horse can recognize other individual horses by their whinnies?

How do we know that animal sounds *don't* stand for words the way sounds in human language do?

How do we know that growls, whines, and barks are a universal code among animals?

To discover whether mares can distinguish the whinny of their own foals from other whinnies, scientists devised a simple but clever experiment. They tape-recorded the whinnies of several different foals and played them back to the mothers while their foals were out of sight. Mares responded—by whinnying back—far more often to a tape recording of their own foal than to a tape recording of a strange foal.

Such playback experiments have proved extremely valuable in the study of animal communication. They are a powerful and direct way to test one's theories about the purpose of animal communication. In effect, these experiments let the animals answer the questions directly for us.

Traditionally scientists who have studied animal sounds started from the notion that each call an animal makes has a specific meaning, just the way a word in English does. Scientists would observe what the animal was doing at the time it made a certain call and assign meanings based on those observations. Birds, for example, were thought to have "food calls" or "mating calls" or "alarm calls" and so on.

But one problem with this approach turned out to be that the same call is often used by an animal in *many* different situations. An animal's "food call" might also be used when the animal is trying to attract a mate. And different calls are sometimes used in the same situation. As we saw with the horse's whinny, one call can be used to mean a lot of different things.

Eugene Morton, an ornithologist at the National Zoological Park in Washington, D.C., decided to take a very different approach to figuring out the code behind animal sounds. One thing he noticed right from the start was that a lot of different animals use the same set of sound types in the same sort of ways. By wandering around the zoo, he was able to record the sounds of a rich variety of mammals and birds.

A spectrograph, a machine that is especially useful for this work, transforms a sound into a picture. A spectrograph consists of a piece of chart paper whose vertical axis stands for pitch—the higher up on the page, the higher the pitch—and whose horizontal axis stands for time. A sound that starts low and rises in pitch would look like a ramp, rising from the lower-left-hand corner of the paper to the upper-right-hand corner. A sound that starts high and falls would be a downward-sloping line.

Morton had noticed that Carolina wrens made a chirping sound when they would spot something like a hawk. When he recorded that sound on the spectrograph, it took the form of an upside-down V. The sound would start low, rise quickly, then fall again. As Morton went around the zoo, he kept encountering that same pattern. A dog's bark is, of course, much lower than a wren's chirp. But on the spectrograph the shape was identical. (If you tape-record a bird chirp and slow it down, it sounds exactly like a bark.)

Morton also started seeing other patterns showing up over and over. Opossums, Tasmanian devils, guinea pigs, pocket mice, wolves, elephants, rhinos, monkeys, pelicans, pheasants, sandpipers—28 species in all—made exactly the same-looking sound during hostile encounters: a rough, low, raspy sound. That appeared on the spectrograph as a thick, jagged band across the bottom of the graph.

Animals had another sound in common, too—a high-pitched whine or squeak or whimper—used in friendly or appeasing situations. That appeared as a thin, falling line toward the top of the graph.

So all of these very different birds and mammals barked, growled, and whined—and did so just the way a dog does.

FIVE

Why Did a Horse Become a Horse?

It is often said that the horse became large in order to run fast and flee from predators on the open plains. But it might be more accurate to say that the horse became large in order to survive on bad food.

To understand why, we need to begin this story about 55 million years ago, when the earth was a much warmer place than it is now. Much of North America was tropical; lush forests grew, and there was plenty of food year-round. Fruits, berries, and seeds were always available to the animals of the bush.

The oldest identified ancestor of the modern horse lived at this time. It was a small creature, weighing perhaps 100 pounds. Its scientific name is *Hyracotherium,* although it's often called by another name it was given by the scientists who first discovered its fossil remains—eohippus, which means "dawn horse." (*Hyracotherium* literally means "hyraxlike beast"—the hyrax is a small rodent-looking animal.) *Hyracotherium* had four toes on its front feet and three toes on the rear. It stood about as tall as a large dog. The males were about 15 percent larger than the females and defended small territories of forest against other males. The males automatically "claimed" as their mates the one or two females whose territory overlapped their own.

All in all, it was as different a creature as one could imagine from the modern horse. The modern horse weighs about 1,000 pounds. Its foot ends in a solid hoof, basically a large, single toe. It lives on grasslands as its natural habitat, not forests. Males do not claim territories but rather move about across large distances and form herds—one male with several females—that stay together as a social group.

Hyracotherium, like many small mammals, was a "browser," an animal that specialized in eating plant foods like fruits and berries that are full of energy. By contrast, the stems and leaves of plants are tough and require a lot of chewing to break down their fibrous tissues and even then don't yield a lot of nutrition. A human who tries to eat these parts of a plant gets almost no food value from them whatsoever. That's because grasses and leaves and stems are built up from a material called *cellulose,* which makes a very thick and tough cell wall that a normal animal stomach

Hyracotherium, *the small forest-dwelling ancestor of the horse, lived 55 million years ago.*

can't break down. (If a person eats a stemmy plant food like celery, which is basically all cellulose, his body uses up more energy trying to digest it than he gets out of it. So, for a person, celery actually has negative calories.)

In order to get any food energy out of leaves and stems, an animal has to have a digestive system that is specially adapted to the task. Some animals, like cows and sheep, are called *ruminants;* they have four stomach chambers, one of which, the rumen, harbors special bacteria that do the heavy work of breaking down cellulose.

Modern horses have the same bacteria inside their gut, but in horses (and also rhinoceroses and tapirs) the bacteria live in a special chamber called the cecum, a long, dead-end alley that joins up with the digestive tract where the large and small intestines meet.

As browsers living in a tropical habitat, *Hyracotherium* and the other early horses didn't require any of this special-ized digestive apparatus. But beginning about 18 million years ago the climate of the earth underwent sweeping changes. The global climate became drier. Forests began to die away for lack of water; in their place came grasslands. It also became cooler: A land that once provided a year-round bounty of fruits and seeds changed to a landscape much more like modern North America. Fruits and seeds were now available only in summertime. In winter plants slowed or stopped growing altogether.

In response to these new environmental challenges, the horse family tree suddenly began to branch out. During this period, which is known as the Miocene epoch, many new branches of the horse family appeared. Some mem-bers of this family continued to specialize in browsing, but others were grazers—they were equipped with the special-ized digestive apparatus needed to cope with stemmy plant tissues.

The grazers began to show a number of other specialized adaptations to their new habitat. They had much larger and stronger jaws, with more powerful muscles, to chew up the tough grass fibers. Their teeth had a larger surface area to help make the grinding action more effective. *Hyra-cotherium*'s teeth were, like human teeth, covered with a

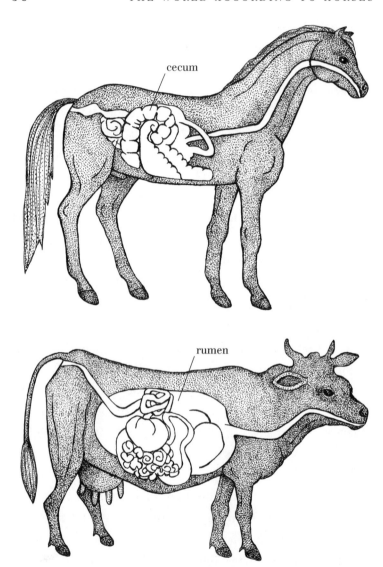

Two ways to digest grass: Bacteria that help to break down tough plant cells live in specialized organs, the cecum (in horses) and the rumen (in cows, sheep, and other ruminants).

thin layer of enamel. The grazing horses of the Miocene, however, had teeth with folds of hard cement on the surface.

Finally, the grazing horses had legs and feet far better suited than *Hyracotherium*'s for traveling long distances over open ground. Many of these Miocene grazers still had three toes per foot, but the two side toes were now shorter and smaller than the larger central toe. The side toes touched the ground to help balance the foot only when galloping around a sharp turn.

These grazers were also considerably larger than their forest-dwelling ancestors. Some Miocene horses, like *Merychippus*, weighed as much as 500 pounds and began to have a body shape that, to our eyes, looks distinctly and unquestionably horselike.

Why should they have gotten bigger, though? The usual explanation—for speed—turns out not to be a very good answer. Big animals do *not* gain much speed simply by virtue of being big. The fastest speed of a Thoroughbred racehorse is about 45 miles per hour. The fastest speed of a racing greyhound is about 38 miles per hour. Yet a horse weighs about 30 times as much as a greyhound. Calculations show that even a modern horse can run only about 30 percent faster than *Hyracotherium* could have.

Being big is, of course, a way to guard against predators—elephants, for example, are so big that virtually no predator even tries to attack them.

But being big also has a lot of penalties in the animal

world. Large animals tend to have smaller populations than small animals do, for one thing. That means a drought or an outbreak of a plant disease or some other chance occurrence in nature that affects the food source of a large animal can wipe out the species in one blow.

Large animals tend to reproduce slowly—it takes 11 months for a foal to develop in the womb, for example—and they tend to have only single births. Small animals have litters and very short gestation periods—two months for dogs, for example, and 20 days for a mouse. So small animals can bounce back far more quickly from an environmental upheaval. If a population of 100 mice were suddenly cut to two, in less than a year it could be back up to 100. If a population of horses were cut to two, in a year it would, under the best conditions, be at three or maybe four.

Finally, large animals are at greater risk of serious injury or even death from a fall. As animals get larger, their weight increases far more quickly than does their body's ability to absorb the impact of a fall. The biologist J. B. S. Haldane once noted, "You can drop a mouse down a thousand-yard mine shaft; and, on arriving at the bottom, it gets a slight shock and walks away, provided the ground is fairly soft. A rat is killed, a man is broken, a horse splashes."

So again, why should horses have become bigger over the course of 55 million years of evolution?

Not all branches of the horse family did become big, by the way. The story of the horse's evolution is often presented as if it were a straight line of progress from small

Hyracotherium to modern *Equus*. But that's not the case at all. The horse family tree was not a straight line but rather one full of branches and many dead ends. In the Miocene, for example, as many as thirteen branches existed side by side. We often tend to think of animals from the ancient past that became extinct as failures that were replaced by "superior" forms. But, in truth, each was a brilliant success for millions of years. Each was supremely well adapted to a particular habitat and a particular way of living. It was only the chances of nature—in particular, changes in climate—that determined which of those branches would ultimately become extinct and which would survive to modern times.

Diet is the key to understanding why the horses that did survive to modern times were big. Modern horses specialize in eating just about the lowest-quality forage that exists in their native habitat. They eat coarse, stemmy plants that other animals shun. How can they do this?

As we have seen, one thing that lets them do this is their specialized digestive system. The other thing, quite oddly, is their large size. You might naturally think a large animal needs more food than a small one, and so it does. But the crucial fact is large animals need less food *per pound of body weight*. This is basically because large animals, per pound of body weight, have less exposed skin area than do small animals. That in turn means large animals lose heat to the air around them more slowly, so each cell in their body doesn't need to work as fast burning food to generate

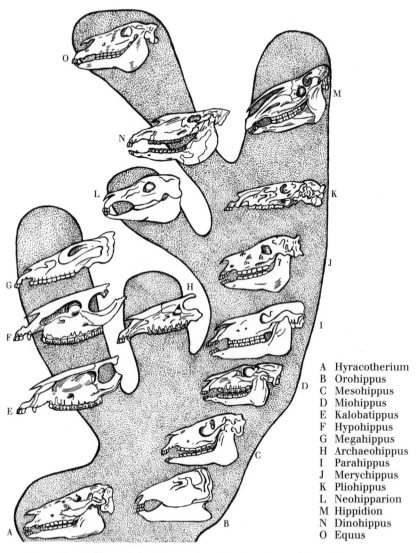

A Hyracotherium
B Orohippus
C Mesohippus
D Miohippus
E Kalobatippus
F Hypohippus
G Megahippus
H Archaeohippus
I Parahippus
J Merychippus
K Pliohippus
L Neohipparion
M Hippidion
N Dinohippus
O Equus

A small portion of the horse family tree, from 55 million years ago to the present. The modern horse is letter "O" on the top left.

heat. Large animals, in other words, have a lower metabolism rate—their hearts beat more slowly and they use energy more slowly. A small animal like the hummingbird, with its extremely high metabolism rate, has to consume several times its body weight each day and has to consume very high-energy food, the sugary nectar from flowers. A horse, by contrast, might eat one-twentieth of its weight each day, or even less.

What's more, because of its large size and slow metabolism, the horse can eat low-energy foods. That is a huge advantage in a world where coarse, low-energy foods predominate. While smaller animals compete intensely for the small amounts of high-energy food available, like fruits and seeds, the horse has the stemmy grasses all to itself. In the world of open grasslands that the modern horse adapted to, being big is a matter of survival as crucial as having strong teeth or a specialized digestive system.

How Do We Know?

How do we know how much energy an animal can extract from the food it eats?

How do we know that small animals need more energy per pound of body weight than large animals do or that small animals can survive a fall better than large animals can?

How do we know what long-extinct animals ate?

Energy is the stuff that both heat and work are made of. When an animal eats food, its digestive system breaks down food into basic components like sugars and fats. The chemical bonds of those sugars and fats store energy. And when those chemical bonds are broken within the cells of the body, that energy can be converted into heat and to making muscles move.

One way scientists can measure how much energy an animal uses is by a very direct approach. An animal is placed in a room that is completely airtight. The oxygen that goes into the room that the animal breathes in and the carbon dioxide it breathes out are measured. The food that goes in is carefully measured, too. Even feces and methane gas that the animal passes contain energy, so these are measured, too. The scientists then add up all the chemical energy that went into the room and all the chemical energy that came out. The difference is the amount of energy the animal used for its basic metabolism—that is, the energy its cells used just to keep running and maintaining the animal's body heat.

One way to think about energy is that it is heat value. Some fuels, when you burn them, give off a lot of heat. Gasoline, for example, has a very high heat value. Other fuels, like pine wood, give off much less heat. Thorough burning breaks down all the chemical bonds in a substance, liberating all of the energy that's stored in it. An animal's body does much the same thing. Not by literally burning food, of course, but by breaking the bonds of the sugars and fats in chemical reactions. The net effect is exactly the same. So the way scientists measure the energy content of food going into an animal and of the waste products coming out is literally to burn a sample and measure how much heat is generated.

The energy content of food is usually measured in calories. One food calorie is the amount of heat energy it takes to raise one kilogram of water by one degree Celsius. (A food calorie is 1,000 times as big as what a physicist would call a calorie; sometimes for clarity's sake a food calorie is called a "large calorie" or a "kilocalorie," which means 1,000 calories.) In a typical test, a scientist might place a carefully measured amount of hay inside what's called a bomb calorimeter. An electric wire running through the calorimeter heats the sample and burns it until there is nothing but ashes left. Surrounding the calorimeter is a tank with a precisely measured amount of water in it. The scientists take the temperature of the water at the start, take the temperature of the water at the end, and can thus calculate how many calories the sample gave off when it was burned. (They have to be sure to subtract out the amount of energy that the electric wire added, though.)

These studies have shown that, for example, a tiny shrew needs more than 35 calories every hour for every kilogram of body weight. A bat needs less than 5 calories an hour per kilogram; a horse less than a calorie per hour per kilogram.

There is another way that scientists can calculate how an animal's nutritional needs change with its size—and also how many other things about an animal change with size. And that is to use the laws of geometry.

It is a bit odd to think of animals as geometric objects, but Thomas McMahon, an applied mathematician, discovered many interesting laws of geometry that animal bodies follow. For example, in this chapter we encountered the fact that large animals are much more at risk of injury or death from a fall than are small animals. McMahon developed some mathematical formulas that explain this. The simplest way to think about it is to imagine that an animal's body is just a simple shape, like a cube. If each side of the cube is a length L, then the volume of the cube is $L \times L \times L$. So let's say the cube is two units on each side; the volume is $2 \times 2 \times 2 = 8$. What if the cube were twice as big on each side? Then its volume would be $4 \times 4 \times 4 = 64$. Its volume has become *eight* times bigger. An animal that's twice as big, in other words, would weigh eight times as much.

Next McMahon asked how much stronger the bones of that animal that weighs eight times as much would be.

What makes a bone—or a piece of lumber or a steel bar—strong is how thick it is. It doesn't matter how tall or long it is, though. Imagine trying to break a match and then imagine trying to break a two-by-four. It's the size of its *cross-section area* that determines its strength. So a bone that is twice as big has a cross-section area only $2 \times 2 = 4$ times greater. An animal that is twice as big weighs eight times as much, but its bones are only four times as strong. As McMahon says, the old saying is really true: The bigger they are, the harder they fall.

Scientists can use these sorts of mathematical formulas to figure out all sorts of things about animals that became

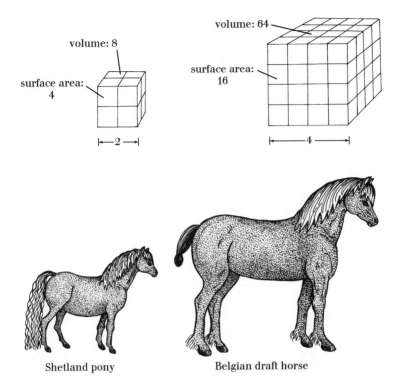

Shetland pony   Belgian draft horse

Thinking about horses as simple geometric shapes reveals how weight and strength change with size. When its dimensions double in each direction (length, width, and height), an object's volume increases eight times, while its area increases four times. A Belgian is about twice as tall as a Shetland pony and weighs about eight times as much. But the width and thickness of its bones have only four times as much area, making them four times as strong.

extinct millions of years ago. They can calculate how fast they could have run, what they ate, even what sort of social group they must have lived in by figuring out how many animals their habitat could support in one spot.

Sometimes paleontologists get very lucky, though, and find a fossil that contains a remarkable bit of very direct evidence. One of the most amazing *Hyracotherium* finds was of a fossil animal whose stomach contained fossilized grape pits that had survived 55 million years.

Seeing Like a Horse

To see what a horse sees, we'd not only have to have horse eyes—we'd also have to have a horse brain.

That's because, as odd as it sounds, eyes actually are *part* of the brain. A huge network of nerve cells form the retina, the layer at the back of the eye that begins the work of turning light signals into an image that the brain perceives. These nerve cells are the same stuff the brain is made of. And they are doing a lot more than just sensing whether light is present. They are calculating whether objects appear as a line; whether those lines are horizontal or vertical; whether they form into shapes; whether they have color. The retina is like a small computer, an outpost of the brain that does the preliminary calculations that help make sense of a jumble of incoming light waves.

All animals do not see the world the same way: There are

many trade-offs in the design of the eye. Good night vision comes at the cost of poor color vision. Being able to see a wide field of view comes at the cost of a loss of sharp focus.

Horses, like all animals, have hit on a particular trade-off that reflects their particular ecological niche—their mode of living in the world.

The most striking thing about the horse's eye is its size. It is the largest of any land mammal. Because their eyes are placed on the side of the head, horses can sweep almost an entire 360-degree circle. A horse can see almost directly behind itself without turning its head. There is only a small blind spot directly to the rear and an even smaller blind spot directly in front of the nose—where the nose itself blocks the horse's view.

One of the prices the horse has to pay for this sweeping panoramic view, however, is that there is only a comparatively small region where both eyes can focus on the same object.

Predators (like cats, dogs, owls—and humans) have eyes on the front of the head, which narrows the total field of view considerably but maximizes the region where both eyes overlap.

Being able to look at an object with both eyes simultaneously is the main mechanism through which the brain can calculate and perceive how far away an object is. This *depth perception* is a remarkable feat of calculation that takes place automatically in the brain. The brain compares the image from the left eye with the image from the right eye, calculates how much they differ, and uses that difference to estimate

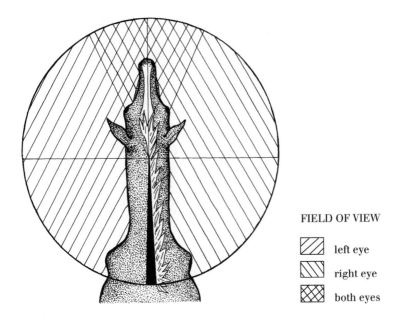

FIELD OF VIEW

▨ left eye

◫ right eye

▩ both eyes

the object's distance. You can get a sense of how this works by holding a finger up very close to your eyes. If you close one eye and then the other, the finger seems to move in relation to the background. But if you hold your finger at arm's length and repeat this experiment, the finger shifts only a little against the background. So the brain employs a basic formula: The greater the difference between what the left and right eyes see, the closer the object is.

Because horses have only a limited region within their field of view where they can use both eyes to judge depth, they sometimes seem to have difficulty figuring out how close an object is. They can be startled by an object, and sometimes, when approaching a jump, seem to have trouble figuring out exactly where to take off. (The blind spot in front of and below the horse's nose also means that a horse generally cannot see a jump as it starts its takeoff: It has to memorize the position of the jump a stride or two ahead of time and negotiate the actual takeoff blind.)

Even without using both eyes, however, horses can perceive depth to some extent by using a variety of tricks. The most useful of these tricks is perspective. When you look at a flat picture, your eyes and brain automatically perceive depth when the artist draws distant objects as smaller and closer objects as larger. In the real world, an object that suddenly grows larger is readily perceived by many animals as something that's heading toward them. Likewise, horses seem able to correctly perceive that more distant objects look smaller than closer ones.

Another price horses pay for their large eyes and large field of view is a lack of sharp focus across much of their field of vision. To have a sharp view, you need to have a lot of nerve cells—as many as 5,000 per square millimeter—in the retina. Fewer cells produce a coarser image, just the way the best computer screens are made up of the greatest number of dots, or pixels. Fewer pixels make the image look rough and uneven.

In the large horse eye, the nerve cells tend to be concentrated where they are the most important. A narrow band at the center of the retina, which receives the light from whatever direction the horse is directly looking at, has the most cells. Above and below this "sensitive streak," the concentration of nerve cells drops from 5,000 per square millimeter to about 50 per square millimeter.

The lens of the eye is another component that determines how sharp the image is. In the horse, the lens does best focusing on distant objects. Horses have trouble focusing on things that are very close.

Overall, horses have a sharpness of vision that, in human terms, is about 20/33. That means that a detail a human with perfect vision can see 33 feet away, a horse would have to be 20 feet away to see as well.

Color vision is another area where trade-offs come into play. Mammal eyes have two major kinds of nerve cells: rods and cones. Rods are sensitive to black and white; cones to color. Humans, and other animals that can see full color, need to have three kinds of cones: One kind is most sensitive to red, one to green, one to blue.

But because cones are so selective—that is, they are tuned to one wavelength of light—they are not very sensitive. To see at night or other times when little light is available, rods are far better. So the more space in the retina given over to color vision, the less space is available for night vision.

Horses have excellent night vision. One thing that assists their night vision is a sort of built-in mirror at the back of the eye, behind the retina. This reflective layer sends incoming light back through the retina, giving the nerve cells there an additional opportunity to detect even very small amounts of light. This reflective layer, incidentally, is why the eyes of animals like horses (and dogs and cats, too) seem to glow when a light is shined on them in the dark. Humans, by contrast, tend to have "red eye" when a bright light is shined at them (you can often see this in a picture that was taken with a flash). The redness comes from the reflection off the tiny blood vessels that run through the back of the retina.

Horses have sacrificed some color vision to get such good night vision. They are able to see some colors but are limited by what in humans would be called a form of color blindness. They can distinguish reds from blues, but greens and possibly yellows are indistinguishable from various shades of gray. That doesn't mean horses do not see green things; they do. But there is no way for a horse to tell apart a dark green object and a dark gray object.

How Do We Know?

How do we know how sharp a horse's vision is?

How do we know if horses have depth perception?

How do we know what colors a horse can and cannot see?

The anatomy of the horse's eyes gives us some clues about its visual abilities. Scientists can examine under a microscope a slice of the retina taken from a dead horse and tell whether it contains both rods and cones and where the greatest concentration of nerve cells is. They can measure the optical properties of the lens of the horse eye just the way an eye doctor does with the machine that measures the strength of a pair of glasses.

But the best way to find out about a horse's vision is to

"ask" a horse. One measure of how sharp your vision is is whether you can tell the difference between a solid gray pattern and a pattern made up of alternating black and white stripes. At close range the two look completely different, of course. But as you start moving away (or—the same thing—as you start making the stripes narrower and narrower), the black and white stripes start to blur together. Eventually a point is reached where the two patterns look exactly the same—solid gray. The sharper your vision, the greater the distance at which you can still pick out the individual black and white stripes.

In one experiment, scientists first trained a horse always to choose a solid gray image in preference to a black-and-white–striped image. They would present the horse with two panels, one gray, one striped, and give the horse a reward for pushing its nose against the gray panel. Once the horse learned to consistently pick the gray panel, the scientists started giving the horse tougher problems. They made the stripes narrower and narrower. Eventually they reached a point where the horse no longer always got the right answer—it picked the striped panel just as often as the gray panel. That clearly meant it could no longer see a difference between the two images.

Similar experiments with birds and other animals have shown that if normal humans have 20/20 vision, blue jays have 60/20 vision (in other words, sharper than humans), horses have 20/33 vision, dogs 20/50, and cats 20/100.

Depth perception is harder to test. But one very clever experiment was carried out by psychologist Brian Timney. As with the sharpness tests, he first trained a horse by showing it two images: a flat panel painted with a picture of a square on it and a panel with a real square glued on top of it that stuck out from the flat panel. The horse was rewarded for always picking the panel with the real, protruding square.

Then the horse was retested, but with one of its eyes covered. This time, the horse picked the correct panel only about one-fifth as often as before. In other words, with one eye covered, both panels looked the same—the horse could not tell that one had a square sticking out of it. They both just looked like flat panels with a square drawn on it.

That confirmed that horses can perceive depth the same way people do—by using both eyes stereoscopically.

Timney tried another experiment in which the horse actually wore 3-D glasses—one red lens and one green lens—and was shown 3-D pictures. These sorts of pictures work because they play on the brain's ability to decode stereoscopic images. Three-dimensional pictures are actually made up of two pictures, one atop the other and printed in different colors. The glasses make one image go to one eye and the other image to the other eye. The two pictures are slightly shifted from each other just the way the images within them would appear to your eyes if you were looking at a real scene. Objects that are meant to appear close are shifted more than objects that are far. Only if your brain is already wired to decode these shifts can you perceive a 3-D image when you look at one of these pictures. The horses passed this test, too.

Finally, Timney did a test to see if horses can perceive perspective, in the way that allows a person to sense depths

in a scene without necessarily using both eyes. Basically
Timney tested to see if horses are tricked by an optical illusion that is based on perspective. In the Ponzo illusion, even
though the two horizontal lines are the same length, the top
one looks longer because our brain perceives it to be in the
"background" of the picture, thanks to the receding railroad
track image that is drawn along with it:

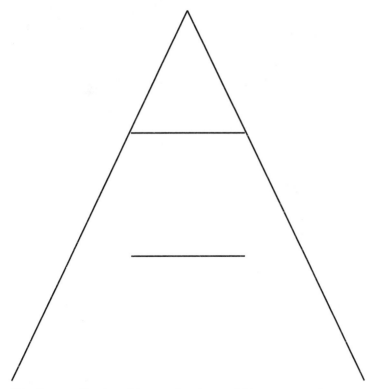

*The Ponzo illusion: The top horizontal line appears longer,
even though both are actually the same length. Tests have
shown that horses are tricked by this optical illusion the
same way we are.*

Timney showed horses pictures with two lines. In one, the top line was longer, and the horse got a reward for picking that one. Then Timney showed the horse the Ponzo illusion—the two lines were presented against a background of a receding railroad track in one picture and, against an ordinary farm scene in the other. The horse usually selected the railroad track picture.

To measure a horse's color vision, researchers have carried out similar experiments. A horse that was rewarded for picking a red panel over a gray panel was always able to tell red from gray even when the shades of red and the darkness of the gray were varied. The horse also learned to tell blues from grays without difficulty. But it never was able to tell green from gray.

SEVEN

Designing the Ultimate Running Machine

If a horse and a cheetah had a race, who would win?

The cheetah—for the first 15 seconds, anyway. Then the cheetah would be exhausted and would have to stop to catch its breath.

A cheetah can hit 60 miles per hour. A horse's top speed is only about 45 miles per hour. But the horse can travel over 100 miles in a 12-hour stretch with barely a break.

Horses are not a lot faster than many other land animals. But they are a lot more *efficient* as runners than almost any creature alive. In its natural habitat, the horse had to cover many miles a day searching for food—the steppes are a place of scarce resources. So the horse needed to be able to run for long stretches without tiring. That means being able to move without using up a lot of energy.

Suppose you were an engineer and were given the task of

designing an animal that was an efficient runner. One of the first things you would do would probably be to see how long you could make its legs. That's because a long leg equals a long stride. With each swing of the legs, a tall animal moves farther than a short animal, which makes for higher efficiency. At the same time, though, you would want to make sure that you didn't just make the legs heavier as you made them longer—because a heavier leg is harder to swing back and forth. And you wouldn't want to make the legs so long and spindly that they became weak and liable to break.

In the course of its evolution, the horse has acquired many adaptations that make its legs as light as possible without sacrificing strength and as long as possible without incurring a weight penalty. When compared to the rest of its body dimensions, the horse's legs are unusually long for a mammal. One way this has happened is by a striking elongation of the bones of the foot. What we normally think of as the horse's "knee" actually corresponds to the wrist or ankle joint of a human hand or foot. All the bones below the knee are stretched-out versions of the foot/hand and finger/toe bones. The horse is, in effect, standing on its tiptoes.

Since toes are short bones to begin with, stretching them out is a relatively quick way to produce a longer leg. But there is another reason that this was the path that evolution followed. The toes are relatively lightweight structures to begin with. The upper part of the leg is much more massive and carries with it a lot of heavy muscles. If the stretching had occurred at the top of the leg, the resulting leg would have been much heavier.

The fact that the top of the leg is heavy and the bottom of the leg is very light has another advantage. Think about swinging a baseball bat the regular way. Now imagine you held the baseball bat upside down, grasping it at the thick, heavy end and swinging the light, thin end around through the air. You can swing it much faster that way. The reason is that upside down, the end of the bat that is traveling the farthest through the air is now the lightest part. The horse's leg works exactly the same way. The lightest part is at the bottom of the leg—the part of the leg that has the farthest to travel with each swing of the leg back and forth. This produces a considerable saving in energy.

Perhaps the most amazing system the horse has developed to save energy is a series of tendons and ligaments that act like springs and rubber bands to recycle energy. Tendons and ligaments are elastic tissues that connect bones. Whenever an animal's leg strikes the ground, some of the energy that was used to move the leg is lost at the moment of impact. In effect, the energy of the leg is transferred to the ground itself during the instant of collision. Some of that transferred energy actually causes the ground to vibrate, just like hitting a drum. (That vibration of the ground in turn makes the air above the ground vibrate, producing the sound waves that make the thudding sound you hear when a horse gallops.)

An ideal design would try to minimize the amount of energy that gets lost each time the leg hits the ground. One way to do this is to make each foot act like a tiny pogo stick. Since the horse has to lift its foot back up right after the foot strikes the ground, building a "spring" into the foot is one way to recapture the energy and put it to good use. The horse uses energy to bring its leg down against the ground. But instead of all that energy flowing into the ground, the pogo spring in the foot sends some of that energy right back into the foot to cause it to bounce up and so get ready for the next stride.

Of course, horses' feet aren't really pogo sticks, but they actually do have springs built into them—springs made of tendons and ligaments. These stretch around like rubber bands behind the horse's heel. As the hoof strikes the ground, the joints of the foot bend down and the "rubber bands" get stretched out to their full limit under the vast weight of the animal. But then the bands start to snap back, straightening out the joint and sending the leg shooting back on its upward journey.

This "springing foot" provides one final energy-saving trick for the horse. If its foot were rigid, the horse would in effect have to lift its whole, very heavy body up and down with each stride.

The springing foot, however, allows the foot joints to bend just at the point in the stride when the horse's body would otherwise be lifted the most.

This flattens out the trajectory of the horse's body through space. Work that the horse would otherwise have to do with every single step—lifting and then lowering 1,000 pounds, then lifting and lowering it again—is wiped out.

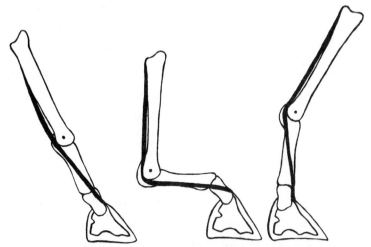

The "springing foot" flexes in mid-stride, flattening out the horse's trajectory.

Of course, no one actually designed a horse. But evolution often produces results that are very similar to what an engineer would design—up to a point, anyway. Why should things work out this way? The answer lies in what biologists call *natural selection.* In every generation, individuals come in various shapes and sizes. Some individuals are taller; some are shorter. Some vary in other ways. You can see this most dramatically in humans. It's not unusual, for example, to find some people in every generation who have extra teeth or who have other differences from the average. The way the genes of two parents combine at the moment of conception guarantees that their offspring will always have a varied and rich assortment of many different traits.

Some of those traits may turn out to be useful; some will not. In the wild, nature is merciless in selecting for survival those individuals who have the most useful traits. Those are the ones who will live long enough to reach adulthood and have children of their own, thereby passing those traits on to the next generation. Individuals whose traits equip them less well to survive in the world will be less likely to reach adulthood alive or to successfully attract mates even if they do survive.

So traits that were useful to the modern horse—traits that were "good designs"—tended over millions of years to be the ones that were naturally selected. Traits that led to a less efficient design were weeded out.

There is, however, one very sharp distinction between what evolution fashions and what an engineer at the drawing board can do. Evolution can work only with the material that is there to begin with. All horses today are descendants of other living creatures. Those were creatures that evolved to live in what were often very different worlds from the ones the modern horse is adapted to. An engineer can in an instant crumple up the piece of paper he or she is working on, throw it away, and start with a fresh sheet of paper and a fresh idea. Evolution works over millions of years, and while it can discard "bad designs," it can't create wholly new ones. No engineer designing a horse's leg from scratch, for example, would make its lower leg a series of long toe bones. Evolution works from the materials and designs that millions of years of previous evolution have left it to work from.

Horses have one final trick to save energy when they move. If you watch a horse walking freely on its own, it almost always moves at one precise speed, neither slower nor faster. The reason turns out to be that there is one very exact speed at which it conserves energy best. Just as a car uses the fewest gallons of gasoline per mile at a certain speed, so the horse uses the fewest calories per mile at a certain best speed.

The reason this is true for the horse has to do with the fact that its legs are like pendulums. If you think of swinging on a swing, that's a good example of a pendulum in action. You've probably noticed that if someone tries to push you on a swing, it only really works if he pushes in rhythm with the swing of the swing. The swing wants to go back and forth at a certain natural rhythm of its own. It swings to the end of its arc, slows down, and then starts falling back on its own. If you push just at the instant the swing starts its return trip, it's easy. If you try pushing at another time or in a different rhythm, it's very hard.

The horse works the same way when it walks. If it walks at a speed that exactly matches the natural swing of its leg "pendulum," it saves energy. If it tried to walk at a different speed, it would waste a lot of energy working against the natural rhythm of its leg pendulum. A horse that walks at the best speed, which works out to about 3 miles per hour for most horses, uses *half* as much energy as it would to go the same distance walking at 1½ miles per hour. Horses automatically choose the optimum walking speed for the best "fuel economy."

How Do We Know?

How do we know what a horse's "fuel economy" is?

How do we know what saves a horse energy and what costs it energy when it's moving?

The best way of measuring these things is by using a treadmill. One of the leading scientists in this field, who did countless studies of how animals move, was C. Richard Taylor. He trained animals ranging from mice to dogs to ponies to walk or trot or run on a moving treadmill. A treadmill is like a moving conveyor belt. A person or animal running on the treadmill stays in the same place while his feet move. It's sort of like the game most children have tried at one time or another (even if they shouldn't!) of running up a down escalator.

Taylor could vary the speed of his treadmill and so make the animals walk or run at any speed he chose.

As the animals exercised on the treadmill, Taylor measured how much oxygen they were using. He put a mask over the face of the larger animals; the mask was attached to a hose and a machine that measured how much air the animal was taking in with each breath. For small animals like mice, he put the animal in an enclosed box instead of using a face mask.

Taylor once even had a person hop on a pogo stick on his treadmill while he measured how much oxygen the person consumed.

By knowing how much oxygen each of his subjects consumed, Taylor could calculate how much energy was used.

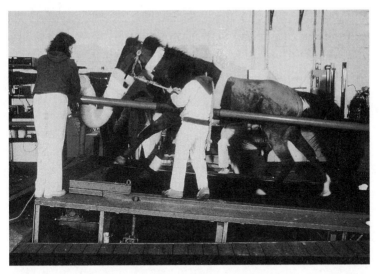

With a treadmill, researchers measure how much energy a horse uses at various gaits and speeds.

Photo courtesy of Howard Seeherman.

He then made a graph for each experiment that showed how much energy the person or animal used at various speeds. The graphs showed that there was always one speed for each animal that was the most energy efficient. The speed was usually different for different animals, though, and by comparing animals, Taylor was able to figure out how the style of an animal's walk or run affected its energy efficiency. That also helped him to figure out what it was about the "design" of certain animals that made them more efficient than others.

One thing he and other researchers found, for example, was that animals such as cheetahs that run very fast are able to do so because they can reach their legs up very high and dramatically flex their backs. That gives them a huge, bounding stride that lets them cover an enormous amount of ground with each bound. But because they lift their legs so high, cheetahs use a lot of energy with each bound and so tire out very quickly. Relative to its size, a cheetah's stride is twice as long as that of a horse.

Another way that scientists have been able to learn about how animals use their legs is by stop-action photography. Today this is fairly easy, thanks to movie and video cameras. But back in the 1870s there was no such thing as a movie camera, and even photography was a relatively new invention. The first photographs took hours to take. A person who posed for a picture had to sit or stand very still for a very long time without moving a muscle so that the picture wouldn't come out blurry.

But in the 1870s new film was invented that could capture an image much more quickly. And the pioneering American photographer Eadweard Muybridge had a brilliant idea for capturing the motion of animals.

He set up a whole battery of cameras—several dozen in a row—and developed a system to pull the shutter of each camera in turn as a horse or other animal walked or galloped past.

Muybridge's pictures were the first to show exactly how a horse uses its legs at the gallop—something that happens so fast, no one's eyes can precisely follow it. Muybridge's photographs also showed for the first time that when a horse trots, there is an instant when it takes all four feet off the

*In the 1870s, Eadweard Muybridge's stop-action
photographs revolutionized the study of how animals move.*

ground. That had been a matter of great dispute among horsemen, and they argued about it for years until Muybridge's photos settled the matter once and for all.

Muybridge took stop-action photos of all sorts of animals, including kangaroos, elephants, pigs, elk, gazelles, and buffalo. Over a century later, his work is still being used by scientists studying how animals move.

EPILOGUE

What We Still Don't Know

The horse is a creature with whom we have intimately shared the planet for thousands of years. Yet intimacy alone does not always yield knowledge or understanding. Many of the questions we have explored in this book are questions that someone living 50 or 100 or 200 years ago would not—*could* not—have thought of even asking. Until Charles Darwin framed the modern concept of evolution through natural selection, it simply made no sense to ask *why* an animal exhibited the behaviors it did. Until physicists framed the concept of energy, it was impossible to conceive of the idea that some foods contain more energy than others—and that this might affect why different animals eat different foods. Until archaeology began to give us an awareness of human life before the age of written records, speculation about when or why or how animals were first domesticated was left to writers of fairy tales and students of mythology.

The more tools that science equips us with to understand the world, the more questions occur to us that those tools might help us to answer. The questions we can think of asking now are still only a small subset of the questions waiting to be answered.

There is certainly no shortage of mysteries about the horse that await a new generation of scientists. How do horses find their way home unassisted? Why aren't some breeds of racehorses getting any faster? What causes the abnormal behaviors that some horses exhibit, like pacing back and forth or chewing wood? What purpose does the playful behavior of foals serve in their development into adult horses? Can horses learn by observing the behavior of other horses? Are some horses actually smarter than others—or do some learn faster than others just as a result of a calmer temperament? How do horses coordinate the movement of four feet over uneven ground and around obstacles at high speeds with such unerring accuracy?

What makes science exciting and rewarding is not only that it is a journey whose destination is the truth, but that the journey itself is exciting and rewarding in its own right. A well-designed scientific experiment is like the shrewdly clever trap the detective in a mystery story sets to get the culprit to betray himself, with all the satisfactions that entails.

In studying animals, this is especially so—you can't ask an animal why it did what it did. Rather, you need to find a way to put your ideas and theories to the test, setting up a situation in which the animal's response provides the missing clue you've been seeking.

How, for example, might you tease out the truth about how horses find their way home? They might use smell; they might recognize familiar landmarks near home that they can see from a distance (like a particular clump of tall trees); they might remember which turns along a trail lead home from having traveled that route before; they might be guided by a mental picture or map of the area around their home; they might even, like pigeons, have an ability to sense the earth's magnetic field and follow compass bearings. It's fascinating even as an armchair exercise to think about how you might set up an experiment, or a series of experiments, that could eliminate the wrong explanations and point to the correct one. A mystery and a challenge is a good place to end a book dedicated to the proposition that *how* we know what we know is as important as knowing it.

GLOSSARY

---

acoustics. The science of sound.

archaeology. The study of past human life and society from its physical remains, such as tools, bones, and ornaments.

browser. An animal that eats fruits, berries, leaves, and young shoots.

calorie. A unit of energy equal to the amount of heat required to raise one gram of water by one degree Celsius. A food calorie, also called a large calorie or kilocalorie, equals 1,000 calories.

cellulose. The chemical that forms the tough cell walls of plants.

Dereivka. A site in modern Ukraine where the oldest archaeological evidence of domestication of the horse was discovered.

domestication. The process by which an animal (or plant) becomes adapted to living with, and dependent on, humans.

energy. The capacity to perform work; energy can be stored in physical systems (like a coiled spring) or chemical systems (like the chemical bonds in molecules of gasoline or food).

evolution. The process whereby life on the earth changes as some traits are passed on from parents to offspring in a population while other traits die out.

feral. Wild; zoologists use this term specifically to refer to animals that were once domesticated but are now living freely in the wild.

foal. A young horse of either sex.

forage. Feed for livestock, such as hay.

grazer. An animal that eats grasses.

Hyracotherium. An early fossil ancestor of the modern horse, also known as eohippus, that was about the size of a large dog and lived 55 million years ago.

imprinting. Social learning that takes place early in infancy.

mare. A mature female horse.

Miocene. The period from about 24 million to 5 million years ago, when grazing animals first appeared.

nicker. A low, gentle sound often used between mares and foals; also used as a nonthreatening greeting.

reinforcement. A reward (positive reinforcement) or the removal of an unpleasant sensation (negative reinforcement) that in training serves to help an animal learn to associate a command with a desired response.

retina. The layer of light-sensitive nerve cells at the back of the eye.

ruminant. An animal (like a cow or sheep) that has a rumen, a specialized stomach chamber in which bacteria break down the cellulose in plants used as food. Horses and rhinoceroses digest cellulose in an organ called the cecum.

Sredni Stog. One of the ancient peoples who lived at Dereivka; possibly the first to domesticate the horse.

stallion. A mature male horse.

steppe. A vast, grass-covered plain.

whinny. A long, relatively low-pitched sound, often used by horses in communicating across great distances.

FURTHER READING

Anthony, David, et al. "The Origin of Horseback Riding." *Scientific American,* December 1991, pp. 94–99.

Budiansky, Stephen. *The Nature of Horses: Exploring Equine Evolution, Intelligence, and Behavior.* New York: Free Press, 1997.

Hart, Benjamin L. *The Behavior of Domestic Animals.* New York: Freeman, 1985.

Hildebrand, Milton. "The Mechanics of Horse Legs." *American Scientist,* vol. 75 (1987), pp. 594–601.

Houpt, Katherine A. *Domestic Animal Behavior for Veterinarians and Animal Scientists.* Ames: Iowa State University Press, 1991.

Hoyt, Donald F., and C. Richard Taylor. "Gait and the Energetics of Locomotion in Horses." *Nature*, vol. 292 (1981), pp. 239–40.

MacFadden, Bruce J. *Fossil Horses.* New York: Cambridge University Press, 1992.

McFarland, David, ed. *The Oxford Companion to Animal Behavior.* Oxford: Oxford University Press, 1987.

McMahon, Thomas A., and John Tyler Bonner. *On Size and Life.* New York: Scientific American Library, 1983.

Morton, Eugene S., and Jake Page. *Animal Talk: Science and the Voices of Nature.* New York: Random House, 1992.

Muybridge, Eadweard. *Animals in Motion.* 1907. Reprint, New York: Dover Publications, 1957.

Pfungst, Oskar. *Clever Hans: The Horse of Mr. von Osten.* 1911. Reprint, New York: Holt, Rinehart and Winston, 1965.

Index